Hastings, 1066 – Words we'd Wield if we'd Won

by
David Cowley
Author of: *How We'd Talk if the English had Won in 1066*

Online at www.authorsonline.co.uk

A Bright Pen Book

Copyright © David Cowley 2011

Cover design by David Cowley ©

All rights reserved. No part of this publication may be reproduced, stored in a retrieval system, or transmitted in any form or by any means, electronic, mechanical, photocopy, recording or otherwise, without leave from the copyright owner in writing beforehand. Nor can it be circulated in any form of binding or cover other than that in which it is published and without similar condition including this condition being put on a subsequent buyer.

ISBN 978-0-7552-1376-4

Authors OnLine Ltd
19 The Cinques
Gamlingay, Sandy
Bedfordshire SG19 3NU
England

This book is also available in e-book format at
www.authorsonline.co.uk

Inside

Foreword	5
Inleading – What if We'd Won at Hastings?	6
'DC' Writes	8
Handy Sayings and Phrases/ Quides	13
1. Simple Questions/ Onefold Frayns	14
2. Expressing Feelings and Wants/ Betelling Feelings and Wants	14
3. Some Sayings	16
4. Kith and Kin	16
5. About the Home	17
6. The Body and Health	18
7. Positive – Winly	19
8. Distress!/ Angsomeness!	21
9. At Play	23
10. At Work	23
11. Discussion/ Mooting, Word Wrestling	26

12. Mechanics/ Workcraft	28
13. Land: Urban-Rural/ Land: Townly-Fieldly	28
14. Weather	30
15. Wildlife	30
16. National Heritage/ Theadish Yearve	31
17. Local Authority, Community/ Stowly Onwield, Meanship	33
18. Church	34
19. Business and Commerce/ Cheping	34
20. Courts of Law/ Hoves of Law	36
21. Defence and War/ Shieldness and Hild	38
22. Travel, Far and Near/ Faring, Far and Near	41
23. Some Things you might hear at Westminster!	43
24. A Few Others	45
Endnotes	46
Appendix: Some notes, Quotes and Dates	47

Foreword

Would that we'd won at Hastings! For a long time, I didn't like to dwell on this thought, to think how England was snatched and stitched up in such a short time by the Normans. Many folk died, but in the wake of 1066 we also lost many words from English – to have French and Latin ones take their stead. Known lost words can however be updated into today's spelling, and this new book puts some of these updated words into a short but handy phrasebook format. The book stands on its own, but also compliments what was begun in *How We'd Talk if the English had Won in 1066* (see p. 51).

As to the outcome of Hastings, I now have a slightly more blithe and winsome outlook! With so many updated words worked out, and now to hand, I look forward to sharing them with more and more folk and to maybe seeing some of them finding their way back into everyday English. That way, one of the worst and deepest outcomes of Hastings can be at least partly undone. About time too – one in the eye for William the Overwinner!

A last note is that although the title says 'if *we'd* won' this book is aimed at anyone who speaks (or is learning) English!

DC, October 2011

Inleading – What if We'd Won at Hastings?

If we'd won at Hastings in 1066, a 2000s school textbook summary about that day might read as follows:-

Hastings, 1066

The Gouth of Hastings was fought at Sandlake Hill in mid October, 1066. There, the English, under King Harold, won a breme and athel seyer over the Normans, led by Earl William 'the Unrightluster', a man who was willing to spill a swith great muchness of blood to fulfill his yearning for the English highsettle, wealth and his own wulder.

The English shieldwall was sorely fanded, but its instanders were tightly knit and it showed itself to be unthroughshotingly steadfast. Hearsome to the King's biding, they held their ground, though the men at times felt a costning to run down after their foes, who sought to swike them away to the plightly lower ground. The Normans could not break through, for the English withstood their horsemen all day, withshoving them time and again. At last it became couth that the overseaish foe was spent; as night fell, those still alive fled the bloody fightingstead into the weald. How could they not rue their coming to these shores, which had cost them so dear?

And so, at the end of that day, when the dead lay everywhere and many Norman and English athelkind had fallen, it was the English who were seyerfast. England stayed unoverwon.

The above is a shortened and adapted quote from The Breme English Seyer at the Gouth of Hastings, *in* How We'd Talk if the English had Won in 1066.

Key to Words: gouth: *battle*; breme: *famous*; athel: *noble*; seyer: *victory*; swith: *very*: muchness: *amount*; highsettle: *throne*; wulder: *glory*; fanded: *tested*; hearsome: *obedient/ attentive*; costing: *temptation*; swike: *deceive*; plightly: *dangerous*; couth: *certain;* withshoving: *repelling;* fightingstead: *battle site*; athelkind: *nobility*; seyerfast: *victorious*

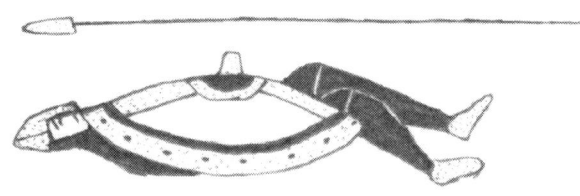

Author's note to the following pages: *This book is first and foremost a handy phrasebook to show how English could/ would look, had we won at Hastings. The first few pages give some background, written by a make-believe character, based on the fascinating thought that some strands of quantum physics actually allow for the existence of other, side by side worlds. A surprising twist, which might be true!*

'DC' Writes:

So, what if we'd won at Hastings? I hadn't given this much thought because I'm a scientist, studying quantum physics. I won't bore you with details of that, and anyway much of what I do is hush-hush. But I will say one thing really important: there are theories in quantum physics that 'random' events at levels so tiny and microscopic that we can't fathom, can lead to changes in the way things happen at a greater scale. Thus, the likelihood that we choose between doing or saying something can change. And when these events happen (and lots happen all the time), whole new worlds come into being. <u>Meaning that there could be many different worlds taking different paths.</u>

I won't say more on the theory, but straightaway it's clear that it means there are a lot of worlds where history happened differently. The team I work with found a way to tap into some of these worlds, and the breakthrough came when we found a 'wormhole' which linked us to another team working on the same thing. They were in 2011, like us, but in a side-by-side world, where some things are not the same as ours. And, we found out, the moment when our worlds split happened some time in October 1066. In their world, the English won, as they say, a 'breme seyer at the Gouth of Hastings.' We talk through a kind of window between our worlds. We cannot go between them (alas!), but we can hear and see one another.

I've written up our talks, and in the next few pages outline some of the main features of English in the other world: how it sounds, looks in writing, and also some of the words they speak. There then follows a phrase book - or guide book - of how to say a broad range of things, covering aspects of many topics.

This is English with few loanwords from French or Latin, for it kept many more words from Old English.

Simple Stuff/ Onefold Stuff

What is it like to hear?

I'll answer this one myself. To me, it's not quite like any accent which I've heard today. Something of West Country English in it, which seems to be the thing it sounds most like. But sometimes it has a likeness to Canadian or American and sometimes to some of the southern Irish accents. But it's none of these really. I gather that this is the main standard speech, and there are plenty of other accents to be heard. The one most striking thing is that the letter *r* is said as in West Country English or North American English. It seems that, as Wessex speech had been the main standard for Old English, and the part whence many of the Old English kings came from, that standard English of today (in this side by side world) came to be based on this accent. This is unlike our own standard English today, which in Britain is based on the speech of London and the SE Midlands, and often leaves the letter *r* unsaid.

How is it spelled and written?

Not the same as our English, and to save making things too hard for you I have made sure that nearly all of the book is in our own spelling. Here though are the main areas of spelling which are unlike ours:

Ð ð and Þ þ: these are both '*th*' sounds. The first are written for the *th* sound in 'the, that and this', which are spelled: 'ðe, ðat and ðis'; the other is the '*th*' in 'thin, thanks and thought', which are written 'þin, þancs and þouht'.

These last two words show up two more things: firstly that

there is no '*k*' – rather *c* is written for the sound. Then, there are no '*gh*' combinations as found in 'night, sight and through', which are written 'noiht, soiht and þruh'. The letter '*c*' is never said as an '*s*' sound. Note also there is no '*q*' and where we have '*qu*' they always have '*cw*'. There are more misslikenesses, but the last one I'll cover is that they have '*hw*', where we have '*wh*'. Thus, the spelling for 'what is the queen keeping?' is 'hwat is ðe cween ceeping?' Like a good many words of Old English origin, these are said in much the same way as we say them, although the '*h*' is spoken more strongly than by most of us!

All of the above spelling mislikenesses are from Old English influence, and though they may look odd to us, from the point of view of the side–by–side world, its us who have the weird spelling, influenced by Norman–taught clerks in the Middle Ages!

The last striking thing is that they often write in a font based on that which Old English was written in. Read this:

Ðe cwikest way to get from heep to ðat field is þruh ðe woods, along ðe old paþ. Go left hwen you've got as far as ðe geit, and ðen its a scopt way down on your left.

For ease of understanding, the rest of the book's text is written in a more familiar font.

The following piece is taken as it was heard from someone speaking from the side by side world, where we won in 1066. He talks about some of the everyday words they use which are different to ours. For this piece only, rather than give a word for word translation of each unfamiliar word to the English we're familiar with, the meanings are described in the same person's words after the main text, under Word Meanings. You may find you can work at least some of them out before checking though.

DC: Can you give some onefold, everyday words?

Answer: Well, you have asked a frayn which may seem eath, but which I don't know how to begin to answer swith well! There's this mislikeness between how we talk which felt weird at first! We didn't know which words you didn't understand in any quide, and now that you have learnt them I've forgotten where all the main mislikenesses were. Still, I take it you mean some of the words I'm saying as I speak now? Alright, I see that's a yes, and that there's already worthfulness for what you want in what I'm saying! I shall go on and you can bewin the words you want.

Going back to the time we first met, I eftmind how unlieveful we thought it was that we had made a findle – the 'wormhole' – which is a link between our two worlds. We had to bethink quickly and carefully as to what it meant, for we'd only weened we might get to look at a side–by–side world, rather than get to talk to folk in one! Now that our understandness has grown we can say that the onfoundness of the undertaking has helped the growness of this field muchly, and has also goodened our knowledge of how tongues can wend.

Now I eftmind a few sunderly words for you. When we ask for something we can say 'I bid you may I have a cup of tea?' or 'I bid you let me in, I have a meeting here'. If we know who we are talking to well, or if it is a child, then we say 'I bid **thee** …' We also say *thee* and *thou* when we bede, which we've learned some of your folk still do. We like these words, for they can feel more friendly. Other tongues have and say their own words for these, as in your world. It seems only your tongue has nearly fully lost them.

Word Meanings (from above):

Onefold: If something is onefold, it's staightforward. Saying things in a few words rather than many is onefold. From Old English *anfeald*. Akin word: onefoldness
Mislikeness: when one thing is not the same as another, this is what the 'not being the same' is called. From Old English *mislicnes*.
Frayn: When you ask something, this is what that asking is called. Understand? – that itself is a frayn! From Old English *fregen*.
Eath: If something is eath to do, it's not hard. From Old English *eaðe*. Akin words: eathly, eathness, uneath, uneathliness, uneathly, uneathness.
Swith: Can mean much, a lot, downright. 'Swith big' means bigger than saying only 'big'. From Old English *swiðe*. Akin words: swithly, swither, swithness, swithliness,
Bewin: We bewin stone, sand, gold from the ground. A way of taking out. From Middle English *biwinnen* (itself from OE).
Eftmind: If you eftmind something, it's in your mind; you've not forgotten it. From Old English *eftgemyndgian*.
Unlieveful: Means you can't believe it. From Old English *ungeleafful*. Akin words: unlievefully, unlievefulness, unlievedly
Findle: Its a new thing you think of and make, or a new thing you find. From Old English *fyndele*.
Bethink: to think in some depth. From Old English
Ween: When you want something and *think* it *will* happen, but don't know if it will, you ween it. From Old English *wenan*.

Onfoundness: The things that happen to you, which you learn from – all are bits of onfoundness. It teaches us often. If you want work, you often need to show you have onfoundness first. From Old English *onfundennes*.
Growness: Not the same as growth, which is more for things on their own. Growness is what happens when a onefold thing like a stone hand axe has led to lots of new and ever-better tools over time. From Old English *grownes*.
Wend: If something wends, it doesn't stay the same. From Old English *wendan*.
Sunderly: Means it stands out; sunderly things are often good, but there can be sunderly bad things too. From Old English *synderlic*.
Bede: Folk bede when they say (and mean) 'Our Father who art in heaven …' and suchlike. From Old English *bedian*.

_____

Handy Sayings and Phrases/ Quides
We now meet some everyday words and phrases which English–speaking folk would be saying if we'd won in 1066. These have been put into topic areas for convenience, though of course words can be used in many contexts. There are some topics which have rather long lists, such as the *Courts of Law/* Hoves of Law and also the *Defence and War/* Shieldness and Hild sections. This does not reflect a particular interest of the author's in these topics as such, more the fact that Norman-French words tended to oust a lot of older English ones in these fields, and so there are a lot of updates for mislaid words which can be put to work! Even so, this isn't the same thing as learning another tongue altogether – most of the bits below have only one key word which is not the same as the English we speak today.

The ordfrims (*originals*) of all of the 'new' words given are updates from known Old English words.

1. Simple Questions/ Onefold Frayns

– *Do you use that?* – Do you brook that?

– *Did you notice that?* – Did you yeme that?

– *What's the difference?* – What's the mislikeness?

– *May I ask a question?* – May I ask a frayn?

– *What advantage is that?* – What behove is that?

– *Was it planned/ considered?* – Was it bethought?

– *For what purpose?* – For what atling?

– *Will you be able to go?* – Will it be that you can go?

– *What experience do you have?* – What afonding do you have?

– *Could you do me a favour?* – Could you do me an este?

– *Has this benefitted anyone?* – Has this gooded anyone?

2. Expressing Feelings and Wants/ Betelling Feelings and Wants

– *Give me an example* – Give me a busen (say: 'bizen')

– *You'll have to try it out* – You'll have to fand it out

– *It's possible/ impossible* – It's mightly/ unmightly

– *You'll have to change your ways* – You'll have to wend your ways

– *If you could wait patiently* – If you could wait thildily

– *Show a bit of sympathy* – Show a bit of evensorrowing

– *Remember me to her* – Eftmind me to her

– *That's unbelievable!* – That's unlieveful!

– *That is important/ unimportant* – This is worthly/ unworthly

– *Something useful* – Something fremeful

– *You're hiding a secret!* – You're hiding a hiddle!

– *Now, that's curious!* – Now, that's frimdy!

– *Don't humiliate them!* – Don't anether them!

– *Not much hope of that!* – Not much ween of that!

– *I'm astonished!* – I'm stylted!

– *Lower your voice please* – Lower your steven, I bid you/ thee (steven rhymes with seven)

– *It's perversion* – It's towarpness

– *This is a special thing* – This is a sunderly thing

– *That's strange* – That's fremd

– *That's all too human* – That's all too werely

– *He/ she's envious/ jealous* – He/ she's evesty

– *I want to see an improvement* – I want to see a bettering

– *You are impetuous for that, but it's too early* – You forthyearn for that, but it's too early

3. Some Sayings

– *Pride comes before a fall* – Wlonk comes before a fall

– *Gently does it!* – Smoltly does it!

– *Opportunity knocks!* – Tideliness knocks!

– *Easy come, easy go* – Eath come, eath go

– *A change is as good as a rest* - A wending is as good as a rest

4. Kith and Kin

– *What's your age?* – What's your eld?

– *Do you have a family?* – Do you have an inherd?

– *My grandmother was 107* – My eldmother was 107

– *A great grandfather and great grandmother of mine sailed to New Zealand* – A third eldfather and eldmother of mine sailed to New Zealand

– *It's a family thing* – It's a kinly thing

– *We're distantly related* – We're farsibb

– *Wedding anniversary* – Wedding mindday

– *Happy memories* – Happy mindings

– *A violent upbringing* – A rethy upbringing

– *Nephew/ niece* – Brother's son/ daughter; Sister's son/ daughter

– *Very likable relatives* – Well–likeworthy kin

– *The human race are all related – we're kin!* – Werekin are all kin: we're kin!

5. About the Home

– *Please, come in* – I bid you, come in

– *Inseparably together* – Unshearingly together

– *A generous helping* – A roop helping

– *What a place!* – What a stead!

– *The bailiffs came* – The wickners came

– *I have my vices* – I have my unthews

What were early English homes like?: West Stowe

– *Do not disturb!* – Do not onstir!

– *Shall I pour?* – Shall I yeat?

– *I perceived/ discovered they were away* – I ongot/onfound they were away

6. The Body and Health

– *Is there pain?* – Is there wark?

– *Don't touch* – Don't rine!

– *She's lost consciousness* – She's lost inheedness

– *High/ low fertility* – High/ low bearingness

– *He suffers from seizure* – He tholes from gripness

– *The joint is broken* – The lith is broken

– *Care in the community* – Care in the meanship

– *A moderate improvement* – A metefast bettering

– *Laceration of the lower leg* – Slitness of the lower leg

– *To do an amputation* – To do a snithing

– *Heal this compulsion* – Heal this underdriveness

– *It invisibly threatens health* – It unseenly threatens health

– *There's some kind of internal disease* – There's some kind of inaddle

– *What are the effects?* – What are the fremings?

– *He suffers from hydrophobia* – He tholes from waterfrightness

7. Positive – Winly

– *That's doable* – That's doly (do–ly/ doo-ly)

– *Very well done!* – Swith well done!

- *That's useful!* – That's fremeful!

- *It was some comfort* – It was some frover

- *That will be convenient* – That will be hap

- *Deeds of benevolence* – Deeds of wellwillingness

- *Yes, that's clear* – Yes, that's swotel

English dress and speech have wended (changed) with time

- *An affable friend* – A wordwinsome friend

- *I'll be very grateful* – I'm swith forethankful

- *You're beautiful!* – You're wlitty!

20

– *My desire is for you!* – My wilning is for you!/ for thee!

– *A happy occasion* – A happy stounde

– *Honourable intentions* – Orefast inthoughts

– *Think positively!* – Think winly!

– *That's pleasing* – That's likeworthy

– *Give him/ her some encouragement* – Give him/ her some forthbuilding

– *If she's sincere* – If she's luter

– *Unencumbered with guilt* – Unheavied with guilt

8. Distresss! – Angsomeness!

– *To have some difficulty* – To have some uneathness

– *He dared to show his face!* – He dared to show his anleth!

– *This is disgraceful!* – This is shandful!

– *Very stupid!* – Swith daft!

– *What arrogance!* – What tothundness!

– *They're inattentive* – They're unhearsome

– *Such impatience!* – Such unthild!

– *Intolerably bad* – Untholingly bad

– *What a presumption!* – What a fortruing!

– *That's disgusting!* – That's wlatsome!

– *Unrest and disturbance* – Unrest and unthwearness

– *It was an excessive action* – It was an overdeed

– *He walked out in disgust* – He walked out in wlatsing

– *What a negligent yob!* – What a yemeless yob!

– *They want to wreak vengence* – They want to wreak wrack

– *You'll have to complain about that* – You'll have to bechide about that

– *What an terrible thing to happen* – What an eisful thing to happen

– *Had been seduced* – Had been forled

– *They have suffered a lot* – They have tholed a lot

– *Don't you have any pity?* – Don't you have any ruth?

– *I feel frustrated* – I feel bewayed

– *A seething hostility* – A seething loathingness

– *Too proud and haughty* – To wlonk and haughty

– *He behaves so arrogantly* – He behaves so uphavely

– *The arrogance is unbelievable* – The uphaveness is unlieveful

– *So miserable!* – So yomer!

9. At Play

– *A walk in the park* – A walk in the eddish

– *A social night out* – A thedely night out

– *You are invited to ...* – You are inlathed to ...

– *By invitation only* – By lathing only

– *It's simply that I can't go* – It's onefoldly that I can't go

– *More frivolity with some comedians* – More lightmoodness, with some laughtersmiths

– *Lighthearted but instructive* – Lighthearted but loresome

– *With little modesty* – With little shamefastness

– *Individual changing rooms* – Onelepy wending rooms

10. At Work

– *Working harmoniously* – Working thwearly

– *A lot of hard labour* – A lot of hard arveth

– *It says it's corrupted* – It says it's wemed

– *They're all present, except two* – They're instanding, all but two (or: all instanding, outtake two)

– *The work is completed* – The work is fulfremed

Much arveth!

– *We've accomplished it!* – We've fuldone it!

– *There are going to be some changes here* – There are going to be some wendings here

– *Make the arrangements please* – Make the dights, I bid you

– *I don't want to put you to any trouble* – I don't want to put you to any uneathliness

– *As usual, they're late!* – As wonley, they're late!

– *Making progress* – Making forthship

– *To build a sound foundation* – To build a sound groundwall

– *You haven't done it in the proper way* – You haven't done it in the rightworth way

– *I'll certainly do that* – I'll couthly do that

– *Who's the manager?* – Who's the workreeve?

– *39 percent per annum paid on time* – 39 hundredths yearly yielded on time

– *Secure access* – Holdfast ingang

– *Wanted: Project Officer/ Secretary* – Wanted: Howing Wike/ Inwriter

– *Is that permitted?* – Is that leaveful?

– *I'm flexible* – I'm litheby

– *In need of instruction* – In need of loredom

– *Send a memorandum* – Send a minding

– *Let's prevent confusion* – Let's forstand shendness

– *Be discrete* – Be sidely

– *What a lethargic lot!* – What a sleeple lot!

– *Break that lethargy!* – Break that sleepleness!

– *Gentle guidance* – Smolt steerness

– *Reliable workers* – Truefast workers

– *What actions are there?* – What workdeeds are there?

– *Operation begins next month* – Workness begins next month

11. Discussion/ Mooting, Word Wrestling

– *Time for a discussion* – Time for a mooting

– *The difficulty with that is that ...* – The uneath with that is that ...

– *I propose that we ...* – I foreset that we ...

– *Very astute* – Swith yepe

– *There is opposition to that* – There is withsetness to that

– *This can't be ignored* – This can't be forheeded

– *It's impractical* – It's unworkly

– *After necessary consideration* – After needful bethinking

– *We should be attentive to these calls* – We should be hearsome to these calls

– *We'll have to change that* – We'll have to wend that

– *That's rational* – That's rightwittly

– *The importance of that is ...* – The worthliness of that is ...

– *Not necessarily wrong* – Not needbehovely wrong

– *This had not been considered* – This was unforthought

– *It's inconvenient* – It's unhaply

– *Showing ignorance* – Showing unloredness

– *What are the benefits?* – What are the fremes?

– *Using subtlety where effective* – Brooking smalliness where fremeful

– *There's overall agreement* – There's overall thedesomeness

– *A swift perusal* – A swift throughlooking

– *I'll have to research this* – I'll have to throughseek this

– *Inextricably bound up with* – Unbreakingly bound up with

– *That's human nature* – That's werely suchness

– *A duty to be done* – An oughting to be done

– *Is it on your conscience?* – Is it on your inheed?

12. *Mechanics* – **Workcraft**

– *It's unreliable* – It's untruefast

– *Control panel* – Wield board

– *There's a fault with this* – There's a wrength with this

– *Well demonstrated* – Wellbeshowed

– *Any good at mechanics?* – Any good at workcraft?

– *Is it practical to use?* – Is it workly to brook?

– *Investigate the effect* – Underseek the freming

13. Land: Urban-Rural/ Townly-Fieldly

– *Urban/ rural deprivation* – Townly/ fieldly forgoedness

– *Leafy green valleys* – Leafy green slades

– *Principal regions* – Headly landships

– *The local area* – The stowly landstead

– *A big region* – A big landship

– *A beach with rock outcrops* – A beach with stonebergs

– *A mountain with curious rock formation* – A highberg with frimdy stone shapeness

– *U–shaped valleys have a glacial origin* – U–shaped dales have an ickly frume

– *Familiar/ unfamiliar surroundings/environment* – Couth/ uncouth outabstandness

– *Local variety* – Stowly missenliness

– *London, English Metropolis* – London, English Elderborough

– *An indescribably glorious sight* – An untellingly wulderful sight

Cliffy shore, Sussex. Near here the Norman fleet landed in 1066

– *Visible at 20 miles* – Eyeseen at 20 miles

– *In the suburbs* – In the underboroughs

– *Tides are a lunar effect* – Tides are a moonly freming

14. Weather

– *It's nice/ pleasant out* – It's queme out

– *Unseasonable snow showers* – Untidely snow showers

– *There was an excess of rain* – There was an overfill of rain

– *It grew visibly lighter* – It grew seenly lighter

– *The sunlight was obscured* – The sunlight was thestered

– *Favourable weather* – Soundy weather

– *Cloudless days are good for solar heating* – Cloudless days are good for sunly heating

– *Drought led to instability* – Drought led to unsteadfulness

– *Adverse weather* – Witherward weather

15. Wildlife

– *Eagle, buzzard, lizard* – Ern, moushawk, athex

– *Beautiful colouring/ colouration* – Wlitty hueing/ hueness

– *Are these edible/ poisonous* – Are these eatly/ attry?

– *A green–coloured flower* – A greenhuen bloom

– *An abundance of caterpillars formerly* – A muchness of

leafworms formerly

– *He regretted hitting a deer* – He was ruey that he hit a deer

– *A rare bird* – A seldseen bird

– *Marine wildlife diversity* – Sealy wildlife missenliness

– *Wildlife Officer in the Local Authority* – Wildlife Wike in the Stowly Onwield

16. National Heritage/ Theadish Yearve

– *The Anglo–Saxon Age* – The Anglo–Saxon Eldom

– *If England had stayed unconquered in 1066* – If England had stayed unoverwon in 1066

– *Declaration for the Restoration of English* – Forthspell for the Eftnewing of English

– *The English Parliament* – The English Witanmoot

– *The Prince may have to wait long for the throne* – The Atheling may have to wait long for the highsettle

– *Nobility was formerly powerful* – Athelkind was formerly mightful

– *Difference between English and Norman royal succession* – Mislikeness between English and Norman kingly afterfollowingness

– *A ship called The Endeavour* – A ship called The Howing

– *Admission is £10* – Infare is £10

(Old English text from Beowulf in insular script)

Old English before 1066: some lines from Beowulf

– *A national institution* – A thedish insetness

– *Remembrance Day* – Mindliness Day

– *Independence for England!* – Selfdom for England!

– *A nation's needs* – A thede's needs

– Lack of a successor destabilised the kingdom – Lack of an afterfollower unset the kingdom

– Who was discoverer of ... ? – Who was onfindand (or onfinder) of ... ?

– A time of transition/ transformation – A time of wharveness/ forshaping

– A precious heritage – A dearworth yearve

17. Local Authority, Community/ Stowly Onwield, Meanship

– A feeling of local pride – A feeling of stowly highmoodness

– Promote a positive outlook – Forthen a winly outlook

– Some felt excluded – Some felt outshoved

– A firmly established local institution – A rootfast stowly setness

– Social Services – Thedely Thanings

– Local Development Plan – Stowly Growness Howing

– Head of Planning Service – Head of Howing Thaneship

– Action Plan – Workdeed Howing

– On Income Support – On Income Fultum

– *Still kinds of slavery* – Still kinds of theowdom

– *Folk customs* – Folk wones

18. Church

– *Saviour* – Healand

– *Sing in exaltation!* – Sing in highbliss!

– *Glory to Thee* – Wulder to Thee

– *Let us pray* – Let us bede

– *Lead us not into temptation* – Lead us not into costning

– *But deliver us from evil* – But alease us from evil

– *Rest in Peace* – Rest in Frith

– *Ecclesiastical property* – Churchly ownness

– *Evangelical Church* – Gospelly Church

19. Business and Commerce/ Cheping

– *The businesses have been merged* – The businesses have been samed

– *Where's this from – what's its origin?* – Where's this from – what's its frume?

– *Previewing the new stock* – Forelooking at the new stock

– *Thrifty and prudent* – Thrifty and forethinkle

– *Have you produced anything useful?* – Have you forthborn anything fremeful?

– *We will recompense losses* – We will foryield losses

– *I pay 6 percent interest* – I yield 6 hundredths gavel

– *A saturated market* – An indrenched chepstow

– *Inferior quality* – Netherly suchness

– *With usury came poverty* – With oker came earmth

– *That's dealt with by the National/ Local Authority* – That's dealt with by the Thedish/ Stowly Onwield

– *We have to pay up!* – We have to yield up!

– *Excellent service!* – Thrithely thaning!

– *A reputable dealer* – An unforcouth dealer

– *Some imperfections* – Some unfulfremings

– *Devaluation of the ...* – Unworthing of the ...

– *It's valuable* – It's worthful/ dearworth

– *He avariciously bought up all of the stock* – He yetsingly bought up all of the stock

– *Profits are up* – Yieldings are up

– *Carbon reduction is a duty* – Carbon smalling is an oughting

20. Courts of Law/ Hoves of Law

– *Is this a reliable witness?* – Is this a wordfast witness?

– *Legal complexity* – Lawly manifoldness

– *In the adjudication* – In the mething

– *Mercy, please!* – Milce, I/ we bid you!

– *I believe him to be guilty of criminal deeds, your honour* – I believe him to be guilty of shildy deeds, your oreworthness

– *Read his statement* – Read his kithing

– *When testimony is given by witnesses, the accused should not speak* – When kithedness is given by witnesses, the wrayed should not speak

– *What is the accusation?* – What is the wraying?

– *That she made malicious, perverse calls* – That she made nithy, bewarped calls

– *This is contrary to what you first said* – This is witherward to what you first said

– *I declare this inquiry open* – I aqueath this befrining open

– *I believe him to be a deceiver, guilty of perjury!* – I believe her to be a beswiker, guilty of oathbreach!

– *He's been a prisoner before* – He's been a haftling before

– *The court believed you were innocent of the accusation* – The hove believed you to be unsinny of the wraying

– *I question the legal standing of that statement* – I befrine the lawly standing of that kithing

– *There are no longer any capital offences in England, thankfully* – There are no longer any headguilts in England, thankfully

– *Cold-blooded and premeditated* – Cold-blooded and erebethought

– *Don't prejudice the outcome* – Don't fordeem the outcome

– *You incriminate yourself!* – You forguilten yourself!

– *Presiding on that day* – Foresitting on that day

– *Collectively guilty* – Gatheringly guilty

– *Was it moved audibly?* – Was it shifted hearingly?

– *Have you not been economical with the truth?* – Have you not been holdsome with the truth?

– *Guilty of burglary* – Guilty of housebreach

– *You stole out of necessity?* – You stole out of needness?

– *I deny the accusation!* – I offsake the wraying!

– *A violent robbery* – A rethy reaving

– *It will be established who did what* – It will be statheled who did what

– *His/ her property* – In his/ her ownness

– *An unproven accusation* – An unbeshowed wraying

– *You incorrectly call this unjust!* – You unrightly call this unrightwise!

– *Keeping a disorderly house* – Keeping an unthewfast house

– *Living on immoral earnings* – Living on unthewful earnings

– *Do you habitually steal?* – Do you woningly steal?

– *He was unjustly held* – He was wrongwisely held

– *Racial prejudice* – Strindly fordeemedness

21. Defence and War/ Shieldness and Hild

– *Don't forget the famous English victory at Hastings!* – Don't forget the breme English seyer at Hastings!

– *This means war!* – This means hild!

– *Army, Royal Navy, Royal Air Force* – Hera, Kingly Shipferd (or Kingly Fleet), Kingly Loft Ferd

- *The Ministry of Defence* – The Shieldness Thaneship

- *Lethally effective* – Deathbearly fremeful

King Harold sights the Normans, *after Bayeux Tapestry*

- *A fierce battle* – A rethy gouth

- *Great destruction* – Great forspilledness

- *The abandonment of sites* – The forletness of stowes

- *Opposition dissolved* – Withsetness formelted

– *An attack without provocation* – An onshot without greming

– *Obedience without question* – Hearsomeness without frayn

– *To give a salute to an officer* – To give a hailsing to an ambighter

– *Overall Commander of UK Army* – Overall Heratower of SK (Samedfast Kingdom) Hera

– *A dangerous incursion* – A plightful infare

– *Shooting/ firing inaccurately* – Shooting/ firing misly

– *Talk to my superiors* – Talk to my overlings

– *Guard these prisoners!* – Beward these haftlings!

– *There were two foreign armies–* There were two althedish heras

– *Conquered, then held by cruel domination* – Overwon, then held by slithe ricsing

– *To reconcile foes* – To sibsome foes

– *Grievously injured* – Tharly scathed

– *Peace agreement* – Frith thwearing

– *There will be better discipline here!* – There will be better thewfastness here!

– *Being sorely oppressed* – Being sorely thrutched

– *An attack of great severity* – An onshot of great swithness

– *Inoffensive townsfolk suffered losses* – Unharmyearn townsfolk tholed losses

– *They're armed/ disarmed/ unarmed* – They're weaponed/ unweaponed/ weaponless

– *Senseless overkill* – Unwitful overkill

– *Their loyalty is with our foes* – Their holdship is with our foes

– *Lower the elevation* – Lower the upness

– *Brought desolation/ destruction to the land* – Brought wasteness to the land

– *Our company fired back* – Our wered fired back

22. Travel, Far and Near/ Faring, Far and Near

– *I'll meet you by the entrance/ exit* – I'll meet you by the ingang/ outgang

– *Long distance* – Long farness

– *Widely-travelled* – Widegoing

– *To travel to new places far away* – To yondfare to new steads

– *Leave at the next junction* – Leave at the next wayleet

– *What nationality are you?* – What thedeship are you?

– *Departures Board* – Forthfromings Board

Seafaring: English Ship, after Bayeux Tapestry

– *Sea port, Airport, Aircraft, Airways* – Hithe, Loft Hithe, Loftcraft, Loftways

– *There's an excess to pay* – There's an overing to yield

– *To the mountains!* – To the highbergs!

– *Descend the mountain path* – Nethergo the highberg path

– *Crossing the border* – Going over the landmark

– *Travelling over most of Europe* – Overfaring most of Europe

– *Resident in the UK* – Homefast in the SK (Samedfast Kingdom)

– *A long sea voyage* – A long seafare

– *A competent driver* – A thungen driver

– *Have regard for other road users* – Belook to other road brookers

– *Concord no longer flies* – Sibsomeness no longer flies

– *Farewell, companions!* – Farewell, feirs!

– *Language translator* – Rerde wender

23. Some Things you might hear at Westminster!

– *The Houses of Parliament* – The Houses of Wittanmoot

– *Call the Prime Minister!* – Call the First Thane!

– *My right–honourable adversary* – My right–orefast withersake

– *Much opposition to ...* – Much withsetness to ...

– *Effective/ ineffective speaking* – Fremeful/ unfremeful speaking

– *To institute change* – To inset wending

– *Such incompetence!* – Such misholdsomeness!

– *We have no power of authority there* – We have no onwieldness there
– *A rightly-appointed official* – A rightset reeve

– *Is there justification for that?* – Is there rightwising for that?

– *Highly perceptive/ lacking perception* – Highly ongetful/ ongetless

– *To impose tough new laws* – To onset tough new laws

– *Inquiry is a duty of the public watchdog* – Seekness is an oughting of the folkly watchdog

– *To involuntarily make a mistake* – To unwilsomely make a mistake

– *Increase in wealth and rise in prosperity* – Upping of wealth and rise in weal

– *Development and prosperity* – Growness and soundfulness

– *Investigate their status* – Speer their standness

– *It's for the Treasury to say* – It's for the Hoardhouse to say

– *A surge in support* – A whelm in fultum

24. A Few Others

–*I heard loud voices* – I heard loud stevens (rhymes with 'sevens')

– *His exit was noticed* – His outgang was yemed

– *With great perseverance* – With great throughwoness

– *Working towards unity* – Working togetherward

– *Pursuit of happiness* – Toseekness of happiness

– *Use discernment* – Brook toknowness.

– *No unpleasantness!* – No unwinsomeness!

– *The eloquence of your speech* – The wordcraft of your speech

– *To speak loud and clear* – To speak loud and swotel

– *Languages tend to change gradually* – Rerdes tend to wend stepmeal

– *They use a wider vocabulary* – They brook a wider wordhoard

Endnotes

There are hundreds more words than those we have met in this book which we'd be wielding in our speech, if we'd won at Hastings in 1066. I have sought to at least give a feel for some of the breadth of sayness (expression) here. For further reading and more words, I bid you see p 51!

Like many languages, English has gained a lot from many of the foreign loanwords it has taken on. In highlighting words that were lost from English, the book has hopefully raised some awareness of something rarely talked about. Although the core base of modern English is still very much Old English words, the loss of many other words which went with these was a kind of cultural loss for English, and has changed both our sayness and how we think in ways that we cannot tell. So, it seems to be seriously worth asking - for all speakers of English today - might there be a potential for an English enrichened anew?

Last, but not least, thank you to all those who gave fultum (support) during the writing of this book, particularly Matt Love for proof reading and comments.

The Author

Appendix: Some Notes, Quotes and Dates

a) Timeline of Notes and Quotes on English from 1066 to today (in the readers' world!):

1066 Battle of Hastings – 'The result was almost instant conversion of England from a Saxon to a Norman kingdom.' Nicholas Ostler, *Empires of the Word A Language History of the World.*

1066-86; by 1086, about 4,500 English thanes had been replaced by 180 barons, of which only two were English; below these were 1,400 middle landowners, of whom 100 were English. 6000 under-tenants included substantial numbers of English. (Figures from Martyn Whittock, *A Brief History of Life in the Middle Ages.*) Some thanes and their followers (maybe many) leave England to settle in Scotland, Denmark, Constantinople, and even around northern edge of the Black Sea.

1100s (early) – 'It is the habitation of strangers and the dominion of foreigners. There is today no Englishman who is either earl, bishop or abbot. The newcomers devour the riches and entrails of England, and there is no hope of the misery coming to an end.'   William of Malmesbury.

1121 – Last entry in classical Old English orthography in Anglo-Saxon Chronicle; further entries in Midlands late OE/ early Middle English until 1150s.

1100s (late) – **early 1200s** – Old English texts being copied and adapted up until this time, as a living tradition. New, Middle English writings of this time still have few French loan words.

1204 – France wins Normandy; feudal lords with lands in both Normandy and England must give up land in one, and follow either the king of France or England only. Although there are other French lands under the English crown, the breaking of this link seems a step towards the later reinvention of English national identity; in time there will be a decline in the strength of French amongst the aristocracy, but also **the ousting of many existing English words by French ones over the following 200 or so years**. So, though lords become more English in speech, use of French words in many key areas – such as law, war and government – wins out over many older English ones, which may well have been last heard on the lips of the less-privileged.

1300 – 'For but a man knows French one counts of him little ... I believe there are not any lands in all the world that hold not to their own speech, but England alone.' Robert of Gloucester's *Chronicle*.

1320s/30s – educated children are 'compelled to abandon their own tongue and construe their lessons and their tasks in French'; The ambitious learn French 'in order to be more highly thought of.' Ralph Higden, *Polychronicon*, 1330.

1340s and after – 'Then came the Black Death: a social revolution followed, and English-speaking commoners [could] move into more influential positions in the cities. French died out in England.' Nicholas Ostler, see above.

1362 – English officially used instead of French in law courts and parliament.

1385 – 'John Cornwall, a master of grammar, changed the

lore in grammar school and construction of French into English, so that now ... children leave French and ... learn in English.'   John of Trevisa, 1385, writing of the time since the Black Death.

1399 – Henry IV is first King of England to speak English (rather than French) as his first tongue since Harold II in 1066.

1430s onwards: - clerks in London develop 'chancery standard' English, in a form of SE Midlands/ London dialect more heavily influenced by French and Latin than spoken English dialects elsewhere. This becomes the basis for Modern English, to which it is far closer than it is to the English of 1066.

1490 – 'some gentlemen [said] that in my translations I had over curious terms which could not be understood by common people, and desired me to use old and homely terms.'   - William Caxton notes feedback on his use of some foreign loanwords.

1500s – 2000s - Scholars add many Latin and Greek-based words: English thus borrows heavily from other tongues, rather than forming many new words from its own Anglo-Saxon wordstock. Nevertheless, Speke (1500s), the Levellers (1600s), and William Barnes (1800s) favour more Anglo-Saxon based English.

b) Some of many French/ Latin Words that came into English, despite there being Old English words for the same idea:
1) 1100s: *war, court, market, peace, treasure, fruit, mercy*
2) 1200s: *obedience, poor, service, heritage, noble, place, prince, change, face*

3) 1300s: *saviour, age, officer, remember, royal, authority, question, perjury*
4) 1400s: *loyalty, public, prevent, solar*
5) 1500s: *legal, conspicuous, external*

Based on the ousted Old English words (and in the same order), the English for the above should be:
1) hild, hove, chepstow, frith, mathum, wastum, milce
2) hearsomeness, earm, thaning, yearve, athel, stead, atheling, wending, anleth
3) healand, eld, wike, eftmind, kingly, onwield, frayn, oathbreach
4) holdsomeness, folkly, forstand, sunly
5) lawly, forthseen, outkind

Note: some loans for things/ ideas ***without*** existing English words would have tended to come in - *with or without 1066* (as had happened before then).

Part of the former Anglo-Saxon homeland: North Frisian duneland, Sol island (Sylt)

If you'd like to know more about our lost words:-

How We'd Talk if the English had Won in 1066

Updated 2011: Now Packed with More!

by David Cowley, Author of
*Hastings, 1066 -
Words We'd Wield
If We'd Won*

266 pages, with background, outline of words (from easy to hard), fandings (*tests*), texts, many busens of brooking (*examples of use*) and a wide wordhoard listed in detail!

Lightning Source UK Ltd.
Milton Keynes UK
UKOW02f2332271014

240747UK00001B/198/P